CW00447099

Celebrity Pets

Biographies, in words and photographs

Of dogs and cats who befriend the famous

With drawings by Linda Thurlow & Dawn Warnock

Claire McClennan

HOLROCKS BOOKS

First published in 1995 by HolRocks Books
PO Box 107, Paignton, Devon TQ4 7YR, England

© Claire McClennan 1995

Typeset in Scotland by Black Ace Editorial
Ellemford, Duns, Berwickshire, TD11 3SG

Printed in Great Britain by Redwood Books
Kennet House, Kennet Way, Trowbridge BA14 8RN

All rights reserved. Strictly except in conformity with the provisions of the Copyright Act 1956 (as amended), no part of this book may be reprinted or reproduced or exploited in any form or by any electronic, mechanical or other means, whether such means be known now or invented hereafter, including photocopying, or text capture by optical character recognition, or in any information storage or retrieval system, without permission in writing from the publishers. Any person or organization committing any unauthorized act in relation to this publication may be liable to criminal prosecution and civil action for damages. Claire McClennan is identified as author of this work in accordance with Section 77 of the Copyright, Designs and Patents Act 1988. Her moral rights are asserted.

A CIP catalogue record for this book
is available from the British Library

ISBN   0–9526944–0–9

'Animals are my Best Friends. I adore dogs because they accept me for myself. And, best of all, they do not read newspapers!'

Zola Budd

CONTENTS

Introduction

I would like to say a very big thank-you to all the celebrities who have contributed. Without their generous response this book could never have taken shape. No matter how busy, they all managed to find the time to provide information on the special animals in their lives and to dig out their photographs, which they kindly entrusted to my care. A minority of the photographs were taken by professionals, and these are individually credited.

Most of the contributors support a variety of animal charities, and in recognition of the valuable part such charities play in lessening animal cruelty and neglect, a percentage of proceeds from sales of this book will be donated to help all less fortunate cats and dogs.

Thanks too to Dawn and Linda for their splendid drawings, and to Black Ace Editorial for turning a typed manuscript into the finished product.

Finally, this book is fondly dedicated to the special pets in my own life: Holly, Bracken, Moppet and Spangles.

Claire McClennan
November 1995

Opinions of a Cat-Lover

You may not be as handsome as the Cream or Tortoiseshell,
You will overflow the shelters and prove difficult to sell.
You may not have the royal blood, like the Siamese
But that doesn't mean you're scaley and ridden down with fleas!
Not as soft as Persians, or a pure-bred Russian Blue,
Your long tail may be missing and your whiskers grow askew.
A stripe here, a zig-zag there, a dash of black and white,
A ginger paw, a brown paw, one dark eye, one light.
There's no such thing as silky fur, your coat's just thin and fine
And as to who your dads are — your guess is good as mine!
You'd never win first prize at the local village show,
Besides they'd be disputing in which category you'd go!
Putting it quite simply, you're a multi-mixed up cat,
But believe you me — there's nothing wrong with that!
No offence to Snowshoes, the Exotics, the Tabby,
The Havanas and the Bobtails, Burmese and Somali,
All purring four-legged creatures, as gentle as the rest
But to many a cat lover, A MOGGIE'S JUST THE BEST!

C.M.

Tribute to a Dog

The one absolutely unselfish friend that man can have
in this selfish world, the one that never deserts him,
the one that never proves ungrateful or treacherous,
is his dog.
A man's dog stands by him in prosperity
and in poverty, in health and in sickness.
He will sleep on the cold ground,
where the wintry winds blow
and the snow drives fiercely, if only he may be near
his master's side.
He will kiss the hand that has no food to offer,
he will lick the wounds and the sores
that come in encounter with the roughness of the world.
He guards the sleep of his pauper master
as if he were a prince.
When all other friends desert, he remains.
When riches take wing and reputation falls to pieces, he is as
constant in his love as the sun in it's journey
through the heavens.

Senator George Veat, 1870

Doodle

A Black Miniature Poodle belonging to
King of Comedy Entertainment: KEN DODD OBE.

Doodle The Poodle – and what else indeed would master of the tickling stick, Funny man and leader of The Diddymen, call his very special Black Miniature Poodle? 'He is the most wonderful pal,' says Ken about Doodle, his fourth poodle.

Never to be left behind, the compact little dog will set off on tour with his wacky master, visiting all the theatres and while Ken has the audience rolling with laughter in the aisles, little Doodle is causing havoc in the dressing rooms, seeking out all the waste paper baskets and gnawing away to his heart's content at all the edges. 'Even if the bins are made of tough plastic,' says Ken, 'we have to make sure they are hidden well away!'

Full of mischief, Doodle's life is one long game. Back at his home in Knotty Ash he will spend his time around the house retrieving any odd items he can find lying around that take his fancy; then he's off to find his master to show off what he has found – but will he let go of the possessions and give them up? No way!

Doodle might be classed a miniature but he's a gutsy little dog and will stand up for himself. If any animal, be it a Crufts winner, star of an advert or even a cartoon dog, appears on the television screen, Doodle will show who's boss! He will bark and bark like mad and try as hard as he can to push the television screen away from him. No intruding dog will ever get into his home. 'Yet,' says Ken, 'if you hold him up to a mirror, he doesn't see himself as a dog – perhaps he's not one really!'

Either way, in Doddy's words: 'Doodle is definitely "The Bestest" and we love him VERY much!'

~

Molly & Ralph

Beautiful Burmese Cats belonging to singer JUDIE TZUKE
Famous for her single 'Stay With Me Till Dawn'

Molly and Ralph, brown and lilac Burmese cats, share their home with Judie Tzuke. Says Judie, 'I absolutely love Molly, Ralph and our Lurcher Daisy – but I'm DESPERATE for more cats!' This is where her partner draws the line and insists they have more than enough to be getting along with. He remembers when the house was full!

'I originally used to breed Burmese and have had four or five litters. Since we now have two young children, I just have Molly and Ralph, but they require the full attention usually given to dogs. Burmese love all your affection. Leave them alone and they are not happy cats; play with them and they'll join in and retrieve. They are totally clumsy!'

Judie was brought up surrounded by animals. 'My family once had twenty-one cats, when our three cats all produced their kittens around the same time!'

'I would always be hovering around the pet shop and any animal I felt sorry for would duly be brought home. I just had to save EVERYTHING I saw in the window! Especially the cats and kittens. I had to make stories up to my mother that they were due to be put down. Once I hid a beagle in my bedroom for a whole week until my mother discovered it! With lots of persuasion she finally agreed we could keep it. After that she rang the pet shop and had me banned from entering in case I brought anything else home!'

'I can't help it but I love every single animal – except wasps! I've managed to conquer my phobia there but still hate them! As for cats – I just couldn't live without them!'

~

© Animals Unlimited

Tasha

Loyal Springer Spaniel belonging to
Theatre and TV actress JENNY SEAGROVE,
Known for her roles in 'The Miracle Worker'
And the TV mini-series 'A Woman of Substance'

'Tasha is one of the most important things in my life' says Jenny.

Named after Natasha in *War and Peace* (a book Jenny was reading at the time) the actress chose the little eight-week-old bitch, attracted by her lovely markings. 'She has one brown and one white leg, looks like a sheep until she is trimmed and often looks like baggy pyjamas.'

'She always knows when she has to behave – then she will be quiet, gentle, polite and totally trustworthy – and when she can let loose on walks, when she is boisterous, noisy and wild although this has been tempered slightly by age. She has got a bit old now for toys but still loves to chase, pounce on and bring back sticks, tossing them in the air as if they are wild animals. Finding the stick is half the fun – if it's thrown on level grass in front of her, there is no challenge and Tasha will turn her back! She now likes the idea of chasing rabbits, more than the doing but at the sight of water there is simply no stopping her.'

'Tasha is a very protective dog and when strangers approach in the street she will become extremely wary, then bark and bark at them to make her important presence known!'

Jenny's Springer has had her fair share of visits to the vet's surgery. When she was younger she was in a road accident. She later had a ruptured leg ligament and a plastic ligament had to be inserted. She suffers from arthritis, especially in that knee but still is able to join in the action and enjoy her walks. As a younger dog she was anorexic; when she was kept away from Jenny for three years by Jenny's former husband, Tasha got very fat. But back with her favourite mistress she soon became fit and healthy again and turned

© Antoinette Eugster

into something of a dustbin. 'She will now eat anything in sight if she is given the chance and frequently helps herself to blackberries straight off the bushes whilst out walking!'

'Loyalty is Tasha's second name. She will follow me everywhere. If I go away for five minutes I will find I am smothered in licks on my return.'

'She has now become a mini-celebrity in her own right, has joined me on several TV appearances, and takes it all in her stride like a true professional.' And if the interview goes on for too long, Tasha will quietly fall asleep.

There is absolutely total devotion between dog and mistress. 'Nothing is too much for Tasha. She means EVERYTHING to me. She is like my soul sister.'

~

Toby

A loyal Golden Retriever belonging to
Singer-songwriter GILBERT O'SULLIVAN

Singer/Songwriter Gilbert O'Sullivan, topping the pop charts in the seventies with his own compositions – Matrimony/Nothing Rhymed/Alone Again (Naturally) – now lives with his family in the Channel Islands.

When he travels to work abroad, his Golden Retriever Toby is left behind to look after the household. But as Helen-Marie, Gilbert's daughter, points out, 'Toby is a hopeless guard dog! He loves everything and everybody. If a robber came in, he would jump up and lick his or her face!'

The animal-loving family originally owned Leo, a collie. Then a four-month-old dark golden brown Retriever with white undercoat arrived, a present from Gilbert's family in England, who was promptly given the name Toby from the film 'Basil The Great Mouse Detective.'

Gilbert handled Toby's training and still tries to be the boss, although like many Retrievers, Toby has the definite stubborn streak. If he doesn't want to move from the car, then he will not budge and subsequently has to be hauled out!

When Toby was smaller, he did his best to wreck his home, destroying a door and chair which today stands covered in scratches and bite marks. A lack of attention or jealousy results in lots of chewing!

'Toby never likes to be left out,' says Helen-Marie. 'He sits on the settee to watch television, loves his chocolate treats and has fun romping in the fields – when a rabbit appears he stands there watching for about a minute, then walks off in the other direction! He loves swimming in the pool, goes crazy over tennis balls and squeaky toys and will sit around all day waiting for the next one to be thrown.'

'He especially loves to come up on the bed on Saturday mornings even though he has a basket in the store room and bean bag in the kitchen, although this is usually occupied by our cat. Toby will lick the cat's ears but even if it scratches and hisses out at him, he will still carry on! He tried making friends with my pony Herbie. Herbie was a bit scared but Toby still tried to lick him!'

Toby doesn't miss out on musical activities either, howling and crying when Gilbert's daughters practice on their violins!

This lively retriever has been in his fair share of trouble. He ran off and chose to disappear and was later found several miles away on the other side of the island and when one day he was locked by mistake in a shed, he crouched in the darkness for two days without a single sound, until he was found!

Helen-Marie sums up what the family think of Toby: 'Toby is sweet and cuddly, he likes being brushed in itchy places and he is very loyal. He is always there if you need him.'

~

Tom

A Lemon Hound belonging to GMTV &
National Lottery Presenter, ANTHEA TURNER

When Anthea Turner first saw the little lemon hound – a six-week-old unwanted puppy – left at the Vet's surgery, there was no resisting his pleading face. Her old pet dog had just died and the tiny runt of the litter looked so hopefully at Anthea that she just had to take him home, christening him Tom, after the Vet!

The tiny hound quickly grew up into a bouncy, boisterous dog. Anthea remembers, 'Tom spent the first two years of his life chewing EVERYTHING in sight – the bedroom wallpaper, my sister's riding boots and bedspread, the lining from my father's hat, the kitchen skirting board. When he chewed the living-room carpet, that was the worst; he shredded the square of underlay and then put the carpet neatly back on top!'

Tom then turned into the family thief. 'His favourite game is to be chased by anyone trying to reclaim slippers, tights and gloves and knowing once again he has got away with it, he will dash to his favourite hiding place, under a settee or behind a particular chair. He has been known to take underwear from the linen basket and present it to you . . . only when you have guests there, of course!'

As for his obedience – 'Well, he once sat down, when Barbara Woodhouse said *SIT!*'

Tom knows exactly how to get around Anthea. He will sit quietly guarding the cupboard containing his chewsticks and push his head under Anthea's arm to let it be known that he's after his favourite foods – egg custard in pastry (if he sees it coming out of the fridge) or chicken. On his first birthday he had his own cake made by Anthea's sister.

Due to continuous jaunts around the country for television filming, Anthea, married to ex-Radio 1 Disc Jockey Peter Powell, has had

© GMTV

to leave Tom in the family home and her mum has become Tom's minder. 'He's the family dog now and loves us all,' she says. 'Tom sits on Dad's knee and puts his head over his shoulder, dozing off, forgetting that he's far too big really. When I visit mum and dad, Tom is very pleased to see me. He follows me about wagging his tail back and forth, dashing about the house. He doesn't lick me but is always smelling at my clothes to find out where I've been.'

'He's a hunting dog by breed and thus loves to track scents. Out in the fields his nose will be scraping the ground. In the snow you can see exactly his route as he goes from rabbits' to birds' to ponies' prints. One whiff of a scent and he becomes deaf and blind and without a retractable lead you end up shouting yourself hoarse! Indoors he has a chair by the window overlooking the garden and fields and never misses a thing. In the evening he is on Fox Watch!'

Without Anthea, Tom is happy with Border Collie Rupert and the two best friends do NOT appreciate other dogs wandering into their fields. If another dog is sighted, then it's Bark! Bark! Bark! Tom's bark being loud and fierce. On the one night poachers were about he promptly woke up everyone in the house and when the ponies escaped into the garden it was Tom who made sure he let everyone know about it! On another occasion, when Anthea's mum fell down some steps in the garden, Tom alerted help by barking and waiting beside her until help arrived.

Joining the two dogs, are the three cats; one as a tiny kitten would safely fall asleep on Tom's back! On frequent nights the cats, Rupert and Tom all sprawl across the double bed totally squashing Anthea's mum and dad! Tom, who absolutely hates anyone trying to clip his nails, will happily bite them himself, often on the bed in the middle of the night!

'Most of the animals we have had in the family have been strays and hard luck cases, including the pony. Tom especially means such a lot to me. He is part of our family. He's boisterous. He's gentle. He's *always* there to greet me when I go back to the family home.'

~

Rudy & Nola

A Red Siamese and a British Shorthair Lilac-Point
Special Feline Friends of
Popular character/comedy Actress PAT COOMBS

Actress Pat Coombs quite simply ADORES cats and is always happy to talk about them. She has surrounded herself with cats and kittens from early childhood.

'I've always kept cats and kittens. Strays and moggies mainly until about ten years ago when I chose to have a British Shorthair. Over many years they have all been special in one way or another.'

Patty has fond memories of Busby, a British Shorthair Blue – who so sadly was killed on the road at eleven months old. 'One day he caused much amusement by walking in with a pair of gent's socks, followed by a very dead de-furred squirrel!'

'One of the most special of all my cats was the much missed Percy ('Persil') who was with me until December '92. He was a huge, beautiful British White with a lovely nature and very funny, very gentle ways. He always reminded us of Richmal Crompton's William.'

The two current felines in Patty's life are Rudy and Nola. 'Rudy, a Red Siamese, arrived when he was three years old via the daughter of a next-door neighbour. He is demanding, very noisy, very loving and follows like a dog! He definitely knows his name, knows who he belongs to and makes headway for any chair I choose to sit on. His favourite place is what we call "The Fairy Dell". There are lots of trees, bushes and shrubs there and a brick-built barbecue. Rudy chooses to LIVE down there, especially when fellow residents have a party! A few years ago, he scampered off to join in someone else's barbecue and returned with a whole cooked chicken!'

Rudy's companion for eight years was the aforementioned, much loved Persil. Following Persil's tragic death Rudy quite simply

missed him so much he began to really pine. Patty tried several 'rescue' cats but came to the conclusion that a newly born would be best so that Rudy could play 'dad'.

'It worked! I chose a British Shorthair Lilac-Point kitten from a breeder. I named her Nola after a character I played on radio for many years (with Irene Handl) and also because she came at Christmas time when I was working with NOEL(!) Edmonds on 'Noel's House Party'.

'Rudy accepted the new kitten beautifully. He is gentle and patient with Nola, although occasionally he grumbles loudly at her antics – which include jumping on his back and grabbing his tail.'

'Nola is a typical happy-go-lucky cat, loving everything that moves, especially silver paper balls. With Nola there is non-stop purring and head butting, she is very lively and was confined whilst still a kitten because of her manic behaviour outdoors! She has a mania for dragging anything that hangs to the ground – for example drying washing – and then having a nibble!'

Patty finds her cats tremendous company and pretty easy to care for. 'They are both very easy to feed. Rudy is partial to raw liver; Nola to raw mince; in the tin range they go for Select Cuts and any odd bits from their mum – chicken, bacon, milk and cream and now neither will touch just water!'

'I wouldn't be without my purring feline friends.'

~

Toby, Flora, Nimrod & Mina

*Four Blenheim Cavalier Spaniels, loyal friends of
Actor NORMAN PAINTING OBE, who plays Phil Archer
In Radio 4's 'The Archers'*

'Toby, Flora, Nimrod and Mina were a family. They were a pack. There was an accepted pecking order and never any disagreement.'

Flora had six puppies sired by Toby and the two lucky puppies to remain with Norman were Nimrod and Mina. 'Yet, after many years – the dogs lived to be fifteen/sixteen – I felt that they weren't company for each other. When I returned from travelling I would find four separate dogs who had separately missed me.'

Norman is a truely devoted dog-lover. His previous dogs were a smooth haired fox terrier and a highly bred Pembrokeshire Corgi. When taking part in a radio programme with Phil Drabble (Presenter of TV's 'One Man And His Dog') from a stately home where they kept Cavaliers, Norman found himself, on his return home, immediately contacting a Cavalier breeder. The result – ownership of young Toby.

His little pack became 'funny and biddable, loyal and boisterous, definitely dog-like and by no means sissies!' 'Toys are beneath Cavaliers. Throw them a stick, shout out the words 'Fetch it!' and they turn a pitying, weary look as if to say, 'You threw it, you fetch it!'

The four Cavaliers were good guard dogs for Norman's country home. They might have gone missing on occasions but always turned up again and had fun wandering round after rabbits, rats and squirrels in their own two-acre semi-wild garden.

'Although they are small dogs, they have feet like cart horses, and sixteen feet end up bringing half the garden in with them! A flurrying, scampering of legs would follow any loud bangs and noises outside as, physically trembling, they would rush inside for

© BBC

comfort. Any form of pampering was greatly enjoyed and all four were addicted to having their tummies tickled! They loved any visitor who would "tummy-tickle" and offer (forbidden!) titbits!'

'They enjoyed the company of each other and rarely encountered other dogs. If they did, they found them more embarrasing than threatening. Along with two cats, all lived in perfect harmony and mutual toleration of each other.'

After full, happy, fun-filled lives the four Cavaliers have sadly passed on yet leaving wonderful memories for Norman. He states quite emphatically that they were his loyal, true friends. When they became elderly, he would make long journeys home to be with them. 'Now that my health and lifestyle make it impossible for me to keep a dog – it would not be fair on the dog – I am permanently dog-starved. I keep a fresh filled dog water bowl and feed bowl always at the ready and friends are exhorted to 'bring the dog.' The words of a true dog-lover.

~

Shirley

Wheaten Cairn Terrier owned by
Eastenders Actress WENDY RICHARD

If you step out into Wendy Richard's garden, do not be too surprised to see various plants struggling for survival . There is one main culprit – a silver/strawberry blonde Cairn called Shirley.

Amongst her trophies, this little terrier has managed to demolish and eat hydrangeas, four fuchsias, a lavender shrub and all but killed off a rosemary bush and each and every plant succumbs to the ritual of marrow bone digging!

When Wendy was filming 'Grace and Favour' at Chevenage Hall stately home in Tetbury, the landowner's daughter's pet dog produced a litter of puppies and Wendy could not resist. 'I found myself heading home with a six-week-old-Cairn puppy which I promptly named Shirley Brahms after the character I was portraying.'

Having a Celebrity mistress soon rubbed off on Shirley and she was soon getting her own share of fame, posing on the front cover of a TV magazine and stealing a scene from John Inman in 'Grace and Favour' where she played the farm guard dog! When Wendy is away filming, Shirley goes along for the car rides and enjoys sniffing around the farm yards where, given the chance, she will chase every chicken in sight. 'She would chase my pet Cockateil, Little Henry, too if she had the chance!'

Energetic Shirley Brahms is becoming more intelligent each day. She learnt to fetch, to sit, to shake paws and to walk on her hind legs. Wendy's husband became her favourite and she would sit in his armchair when he was out. Knowing he was the boss, Shirley would obey. But with Wendy – no chance! 'Shirley walks all over me and the only way I can get her to do anything is to mention and to produce FOOD! She loves her treats, fresh food and vegetables and all kinds of fruit, although she will turn her nose up at an

orange . . . Recently I caught her stealing John Inman's roast beef sandwich – complete with horseradish – from his shopping bag!'

'One of Shirley's latest crazes is to sit on the pub stool waiting for a handful of ice, crunching the cubes up in her teeth and playing with them on the pub floor. Making a true spectacle of herself, she will wait until everyone is watching, put her head down, her rear in the air, then fall flat on her back waiting to be tickled. She's a true strumpet!'

'Chewing is another favourite pastime. She has managed to eat her way through rubber toys, her rubber rat has now lost its squeak and most of its tail; socks are a great favourite; so too the contents of my handbag – my chewed diary ended up coverless! The contents of waste paper baskets are frequently strewn half chewed all over the floor and shredding kleenex she finds great fun. Her chewing highlight was to demolish my expensive trainers, not to mention chewing the flex of an art deco lamp, sending it crashing to the floor!'

'Nevertheless, Shirley is a true and loyal friend. As I have no children, Shirley is my "baby"!'

Bonnie

Black-and-white cat belonging to
Author & Astronomer Dr PATRICK MOORE CBE

Approximately seventeen years ago, a small black and white kitten entered the Sussex country garden of Astronomer Patrick Moore, he who for many years has presented his own TV programme 'The Sky At Night'. 'She said quite clearly that she was a black and white kitten without a home,' he says. 'I was a home without a black and white kitten; this made no sense. One can't argue with logic like that, and I did not try. So Bonnie took over!'

Bonnie had found a new master who has always loved cats. As a boy Patrick owned a lovely ginger cat who lived to the great age of twenty and a half years – and a home where there was fish, fish and more fish (specifically cod) on the menu. Bonnie was happy. She had found a beautiful rose garden in Patrick's seaside home, in which to curl up and snooze under the sun and indoors a look-out spot on top of Patrick's observatory!

Patrick says of Bonnie, 'She is not really "special" – except, of course, to me! Bonnie is gentle and friendly and has a loud purr. But she can be quite skittish!'

'She has one habit of which I cannot break her. I have a fax machine which receives messages from all over the world. Because it is in the bay window of my study overlooking the rose garden and is warm, Bonnie WILL sit on it. She has become somewhat notorious for doing this. This promptly turns it off! I had one recent telephone call from New Zealand – an anxious voice saying, "I am trying to send you a fax. Will you PLEASE take your cat off the machine!" I took Bonnie off and the message came through!' He adds, 'It isn't a question of *The Cat sat on the Mat*; more a case of *The Cat sat on the Fax!* A somewhat perverse cat – that's my Bonnie!'

~

Tarka

Black Labrador owned by Lady Becky Blandford,
Married to James Churchill, the Marquess of Blandford
(Son of the Duke of Marlborough of Blenheim Palace)

Becky, The Marchioness of Blandford, is known for her great love of horses and is now enjoying a new life as an amateur jockey with a busy riding career. Her dogs, however, are still very much an important part of her life. She chooses to own Black Labradors because of their gentleness with children and the fact that they are 'good fun dogs.'

'My black Labrador Tarka, who I named after the otter, is loyal, stuck up and spoilt! When I'm driving along Tarka sits in the front and looks down her nose at people as though they are a piece of muck!' she says. 'It is quite embarrassing!'

'It is not just car travelling that Tarka enjoys. She is a dog who absolutely ADORES flying! If the door of a helicopter is open, in she will jump and sit patiently waiting for take off!'

'Tarka used to love being my small son's pony! When he was tiny he rode on her back and she would walk around with him laughing on top of him. Very occasionally she'd have a gentle roll and off he'd fall, giggling.'

'She is just so spoilt,' says her mistress, 'she gets her own way and does whatever she wants! Having licked all the icing off one of my mother's cakes that was sitting enticingly on a plate on the kitchen table, she then left the cake fully intact still on the plate. When my mother returned she thought she had gone mad and forgotten to ice the cake, while Tarka sat guiltily in the corner, licking her lips, guilt written all over her face!'

Becky owns four Black Labradors: Tarka, Seal, Spider and Otter. Seal is Tarka's best friend and the two dogs sleep on top of each other! With the help of friend Barny, Tarka managed to produce

seven adorable puppies. Spider and Otter were the two that Becky could not resist and they therefore joined the family while the others went off to good homes.

All Becky's dogs love chasing balls, chasing cats and the long walks in the Oxfordshire fields on the Cotswold borders with their mistress. While Becky enjoys the walks to keep fit, Tarka will catch rabbits and insists on carrying them home. She also loves to swim and Becky can never keep her out of the water. But rain is another matter. 'Tarka hates getting up in the morning and when it is raining, she does not look out of the window to check – she *just knows*. Then she will stay asleep all day and not bother to get up at all! All the dogs sleep on my bed, Tarka with her head on the pillow. If she wants something she will butt me with her nose very hard until she gets it!'

Becky knows no fear when she is surrounded by her dogs. Tarka is an excellent guard dog and will always protect her mistress. If anyone approaches the car, she will bark like mad. She has also been known to bite people on motorbikes!

Tarka means everything to Becky. She has given her several anxious moments though, suffering a couple of 'awful' experiences. "When Tarka was two years old she chased a pigeon across a busy London road. I have never heard such a noise, as she collided into car wheels. Luckily she only did damage to one leg, which is fine now, but Tarka's name changed to "Zippy" for a while as all her stitches criss-crossed up her leg! On another occasion I found her in the middle of a field having convulsions, and it was pretty much touch and go for a while.'

However, Tarka is now fully fit and apart from wanting to eat Becky's budgies, she is the most 'wonderful dog around'! When Becky speaks of her Black Labradors she says: 'I think they are the best friends anyone could ever have. I couldn't imagine life without them.'

~

Smokey

A 'faithful, daft old dog!' belonging to Actor
STAN RICHARDS, Emmerdale's famous
Yorkshireman 'Seth'

Stan Richards, just like his famous television character Seth Armstrong from 'Emmerdale', speaks of his beloved old dog Smokey with an awful lot of tongue in cheek.

'Smokey's been a complete nuisance for fifteen years but we dread the day we lose him! He's as daft as myself, my wife, my three sons, three daughters and all the grandchildren put together – mind you, he has to be to put up with us!'

Smokey is, in Stan's words, 'a mixed up variety of dog with beautiful gold, fading to silver fur which just never stops moulting.' Stan well remembers the day when his son discovered the seven week old tiny pup on a local farm. He was about to be put to sleep as nobody wanted him – but the Richards family definitely did and Smokey never looked back. Chuckling Stan says he has: 'absolutely no control over the animal! Smokey has trained us to fit into his idea of life. He terrifies me and I do as I'm told.'

'When Smokey has the chance he will go off and get himself lost. Then he'll hide and sit laughing at us trying to find him! He costs me a fortune in vet's bills, keeps me on the verge of bankruptcy and sits grinning at me at a grand age when he should be long gone!'

Stan's wife Sue has always been Smokey's favourite – she is in charge of the larder. 'He's an absolute glutton, that Smokey. He eats like a Trojan, eating, biting and chewing anything and everything including people and the budgies!'

The whole family bow to Smokey's every whim. 'We always make sacrifices for Smokey and I always will whilst he is still here,' says his master. For during his lifetime Smokey has done his master proud. He joined Stan in Emmerdale in 1981 and for several years

featured as Seth's own dog. He had quite a few important story lines, performing them all well, enjoying the filming in and around The Woolpack Inn. He became a favourite and a star amongst the Emmerdale cast and earned his keep in tins of dog food. At a grand age he retired from playing his role of Seth's dog.

When Smokey's time comes, Stan will never forget his lovable friend. Man's best friend? 'No contest,' laughs Stan. 'You've obviously met the family!'

'I have Smokey preserved for ever on video, alongside Rin Tin Tin and Lassie! What more could I ask for?'

~

Minnie & Mouse

Two little cats belonging to
Former 'Emmerdale' Actress KATE DOVE

Kate Dove, who played Elizabeth Pollard in Yorkshire Television's popular soap 'Emmerdale', has found that whenever her house is without a cat, one will suddenly turn up and make itself at home.

'My husband Alasdair used to have Siamese cats in his family and I met the last two, Orlando and Toto. Toto was a Lilac point, she lived to a very grand age, and my love affair with cats began with her!'

Then along to Kate's home, there appeared suddenly on her doorstep a Ginger Tom. She says: 'My husband was appearing in a show at that time – *Equus* – so this new ginger feline was promptly given the name and took up residence. Equus was very great friends with our Old English Sheepdog Puccini (Poo). They would go on food raids together, Equus would get up to the box of chocolates or whatever and throw them down to a waiting dog! They once demolished a bowl of fruit that way and two pork chops from under the lighted grill of the oven – yes, when it was on!'

Poo died a year before his partner-in-crime and when Equus passed on seven years ago, there became a gap in the household. Two little tabby coloured moggies, Minnie and Mouse from a village just outside York, were quick to step over the threshold.

Minnie (the Minx) has the short coat and Mouse (the very shy one) has longer, more fluffy fur, but despite being sisters these two have very different temperaments.

'Minnie is very gregarious,' says Kate. 'She loves men especially. She is very curious about everything and loves to climb as high as she can, especially on my husband's shoulders to get a better look at everything and everyone.

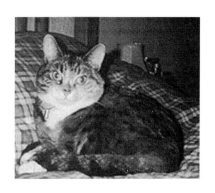

'Mouse, on the other hand, is extremely reserved. She takes a long time to get to know people. She always comes to tell us when she thinks it is time for bed and it's then that she likes to show and receive affection. She's also the one who wakes us up, knocking things off the chest of drawers and stomping around! If she thinks breakfast is going to be late, she "talks" very loudly!'

The two cats together have fun getting into mischief. 'They have caught two birds in the past and brought them into the house, but they don't know what to do with them! Both birds were uninjured and the "girls" were seemingly quite relieved to let us release them!'

Both love the master bed to sleep on; another favourite place being the back of the sofa where they will push the blind aside to see what is going on in the street! Kate says when they are feeling active they love to go 'tobogganing in my shoes on our wooden floor' and then they are happy to settle down to a meal of 'anything expensive.' 'A tin of game and hare goes down a treat,' she says, 'but the portions are so small they demand it is followed up with a portion of cat biscuits!'

Minnie and Mouse have a fascinating relationship. 'Like sisters the world over, they go through moods with each other. They can be the best of friends one day and bitter enemies the next. Curiously it is Mouse, the shy one, who repels invaders. She can be very bold if she thinks one of the neighbouring cats is coming in for a visit. Minnie was great friends with the cat next door, who would often come in to play before he moved away – Mouse would watch and then just sulk!'

'However, I'm just grateful Minnie and Mouse deign to live with me. Although they do cost me a small fortune. Minnie had very bad wind once and we thought she was seriously ill. By the time we reached the vet early on a Sunday morning, the wind had passed! A very expensive bout of flatulence, that!'

~

Bobby & Sika

Two Springer Spaniels belonging to
LORD & LADY MONTAGU and Family of Beaulieu

Toast covered with Kiwi Fruit Spread! That is the favourite treat of Bobby and Sika, two friendly Springer Spaniels who live in stately Beaulieu Palace in Hampshire, home to Lord and Lady Montagu and family and the famous Beaulieu Motor Museum. They are dogs who will eat practically anything.

Jonathan, Lord Montagu's son, explains: 'Bobby has become very clever with any guests to the Palace, trying to get them to feed him titbits. One day we were having dinner on a table with a large table cloth. At the end of the meal Bobby rushed out dragging the tablecloth with our lunch, all the way down the corridor with the plates balancing on his back for quite a few seconds!' Other tasty titbits sought after, have been Jonathan's other pets! 'We once had a goldfish which they wanted to eat, and rats which they enjoyed chasing around the house!'

'Both of them love me – at meal times. I wonder why!' he says. 'But out shooting, my father is their favourite.'

Lord Montagu has always kept either Labradors or Springer Spaniels because of their suitability as working dogs on shoots. Bobby and Sika, named after a breed of deer found in the New Forest, both came originally from a breeder in Devon. They were both trained by a dog trainer in the Midlands. 'Although,' says Jonathan, 'you wouldn't guess it! They have both ended up quite disobedient. But we do encourage them to watch Crufts on television!'

Bobby is the boisterous one; Sika is quite calm but he has a very stubborn streak when something has caught his interest, and he always manages to find some reason why not to return to his master! They love their walks beside the river, chasing the ducks and swimming in the water after them. Sika especially loves 'hide and seek' in the river reeds but Jonathan points out that 'seek on the

© Jonathan Montagu

human's part is rather limited since the reeds are part-way into the water!' Both have begun the habit of wandering off into the bushes and becoming increasingly difficult to find!

'A year ago we lost Sika in our grounds. After much searching until eleven o'clock at night, we gave up and went to bed. At four in the morning we suddenly heard barks outside. We all searched but could find nothing and the barking stopped. Back to bed and an hour later the barking began again! Finally we heard a whining near our swimming pool and soon found young Sika trapped under the swimming-pool chalet. With the aid of a spade we finally managed to dig him out. He was VERY pleased to have some food having been there for more than twelve hours!'

These home-loving Springers have now managed to get their own way with regards to sleeping in baskets inside the Palace House. Lord Montagu tried putting them in outside kennels but they weren't having any of that! They barked and barked all through the night, depriving the family of any chance of sleep.

Whenever the family return having been away, even for a short time, there is a mass of wagging tails and a few chewed baskets. 'We have to buy baskets once a year or more as they chew them and likewise they go through bedding very quickly.' Jonathan admits large amounts of money are spent on the pair and life adjusts to accommodate them. 'We go on holiday only if somebody can look after them twenty-four hours a day.'

But the Montagu Family reckon Bobby and Sika are worth more than any sacrifices. 'Our dogs show many human feelings. Bobby and Sika are very good company – friends to be with.'

~

Jasper & Charlie

Two handsome Golden Retrievers belonging to
PETER SHILTON, football player, manager and
Former England goalkeeper

'Loyal, Lovable and Great Company,' is how Peter Shilton and his family describe their two Golden Retrievers Jasper, aged nine, and Charlie, aged four.

The Shiltons have always kept dogs and these, their present family pets, like nothing better than swimming, chasing rabbits and their long country walks in the Devon countryside, having moved here when their master became Manager of Plymouth Argyle Football Club.

'Jasper and Charlie are the best of friends. They are very protective of their home and they play together continually. They are our friends and companions.'

~

Malcolm

An Alsation-Collie Cross owned by
Bubbly 'Bucks Fizz' Singer
Turned TV Presenter, CHERYL BAKER

'He's like my son, if you like,' says Cheryl, describing her beloved black-and-tan Alsatian-cross Malcolm. He joined his mistress as a tiny ball of fluff when he was twelve weeks old, from a friend's dog's litter and Cheryl has been mad about him ever since.

'A human being would never be as trusting or as loyal as this dog,' Cheryl says, and in return she considers her Malcolm before almost anything else. 'I organize hotels that take dogs if I have to work away or else he will go to my mum and dad. I love to take holidays in the United Kingdom – then Malcs can come too.'

Cheryl has had several dogs – always mongrels – and Malcolm has turned out so intelligent she finds he impresses people without ever being taught! She found his basic training very easy and she is now proud to say he has become an obedient, loyal, gentle dog, looking on his mistress with the utmost trust. If Cheryl's husband Steve ever dares to tell Malcs off, a timid Malcolm is off like a shot to hide behind Cheryl's legs!

As a television presenter Cheryl has appeared in a variety of programmes, including those on good food, but where her dog is concerned she says, 'Malcolm likes tripe but basically eats anything that smells revolting! He is not greedy and does not scavenge around the dinner table but when no-one is looking, like any dog, he will take his chance. Grabbing hold of a mouthful of food, he will carry it into the lounge and enjoy it with relish on the carpet. Then act the innocent!'

'Malcs would run for England if he could! Out on the playing fields he will tear around, loving a game with other dogs, "fetching", and his favourite game: chasing sticks and balls. He also enjoys his woodland walks, stopping for a good sniff around the trees and if

he gets the chance to chase a fox, then Malcs is off! If he can grab a quick swim in the water he is in his element.'

Malcolm does a wonderful job for Cheryl in guarding her house. 'He has the most ferocious bark and would never let a stranger into the house or garden. However, if I let a stranger in, then Malcs will run away!'

'On my return from work, Malcolm is ecstatic. He will yelp, jump up and down, fetch his ball and the fun begins.' Malcolm is a dog totally loved to pieces.

~

Gypsy

A wonderful-natured Rottweiler owned by
LESLIE THOMAS, best-selling Author of
The Virgin Soldiers *and* Arrivals and Departures

Author Leslie Thomas has Gypsy – a nine-year-old Rottweiler who is his 'marvellous companion' and 'excellent watchdog'.

Previously living in a fairly remote house and being often away, he needed a guard dog. So Gypsy – named after a gypsy Leslie had met! – aged seven months joined the household, 'simply because I just liked the look of her.'

'She has proved to be perfect at her job. She is very obedient, knows exactly that I am the boss, is very calm (unless she knows she is going to have her toenails clipped!), lovable and loyal. Once she knows people are supposed to be in the house, she will make a big fuss of them and is wonderful with strangers once she has got to know them.'

Gypsy especially loves Leslie's wife Diana. 'This dog knows she gets fed once a day by my wife but she is forever optimistic and will carry around any bowl or piece of crockery just as a hint that it could well be dinner time! Rattle a tube of Smarties and Gypsy is your instant best friend – she has become somewhat of a serious Smartie addict and will jump up and take them off the end of my nose!'

Guard dog she may well be, but this Rottweiler cannot get enough pampering. 'She sleeps on a rug on the landing outside the bedroom and if she sees holiday suitcases appearing, she will be a very glum dog and go off into a deep sulk!'

'Her greatest fun is swimming in the River Avon, which passes the bottom of her garden, or madly chasing rabbits, pigeons, pheasants and most especially squirrels round and round the garden and in the Cathedral grounds, where she goes for her walks. She will offer all

the neighbouring cats the greatest of respect and gets on well with our other dog – an elderly dachschund.'

Leslie has no bad stories to tell about this lovely dog. 'Gypsy is the opposite of all the Rottweilers who feature in the press. She has a wonderful nature. The only problem was when, as a young bitch, she disappeared to elope in the company of the family's basset hound (the late, much loved Furlong) who just so happened to be seriously in love with her! I did not dare to think what the results of any union might have been – fortunately there were none!'

~

Whisky & Soda

A pair of Norfolk Terriers belonging to
The Governor of Hong Kong, CHRIS PATTEN
And his wife Lavender

When the time came to choose a dog, Chris Patten, the Governor of Hong Kong, and his wife Lavender picked two sandy brown, rough long-haired Norfolk Terriers because of 'their neat compactness and their pleasant little natures'.

Lavender admits: 'The terrible twosome Whisky and Soda are proving to be very friendly little dogs, naughty but quite charming and good fun. They are totally and absolutely the best of friends, chasing, rolling and mock fighting. Whisky the dog, being a month older, is the braver of the two; Soda the bitch, gets slightly frightened and overwhelmed by lots of strange people.' With all the bustle at Government House, Lavender still manages to find time to fit in the dog-walking, grooming and feeding. 'The two dogs are quite fussy eaters although a favourite at the moment is cheese straws!'

The whole Patten family, including Whisky, were in despair when, having only just settled in Hong Kong, Soda got herself lost for four days. The British tabloid papers were filled with the news that Soda could well end up as 'delicacy of the day' in a local restaurant. But the puppy returned, bedraggled and exhausted but wagging her tail, responding to a tumultuous welcome by Whisky.

The two Terriers have quite won over all the staff at Government House. They have become real 'House' dogs. They sit together in the front hall most of the day and watch everything that is going on, greeting everyone on their arrival. Since it is also an office, they are kept as busy as the staff – their wagging tails exerting into overdrive to keep up with a real British 'Norfolk' welcome.

~

© Sally Anne Thompson Animal Photography

© Sally Anne Thompson Animal Photography

Mollie

Little Black Scottie owned by ERNIE WISE OBE

Ernie Wise, half of the British double act Morecambe and Wise has a little black Scottie, Mollie – a dog with the most incredible hearing; prospective intruders beware! She can bark, bark and BARK! A 7.30 a.m. bark heralds the milkman, the eight o'clock bark the paperboy and if barking starts in the middle of the night Ernie knows there are squirrels about.

'We like the small breeds, especially Scotties, for their spirit. Their fur feels good but with such short legs they do tend to get rather wet in the long grass and drying them is a necessity.'

'Boots' was Ernie's first Scottie, bought from a pet shop in Weymouth; then came Charlie, the poodle whom he adopted when his original owner was emigrating to Australia, and a few years ago Mollie, aged one, was adopted from the RSPCA.

'Mollie is certainly no lap dog. Send her outside and she turns into a terror! She'll chase cars, she'll chase bikes, she'll chase dogs three times her size and attack, she'll chase cats and birds – there is no discrimination. Everything is hounded straight out of the garden whether they be delivery man, dustman or pigeon!'

'Take her back into the house and she is a little softie. She's not keen on being picked up but she does love to sit and watch television. If a dog or bird appears, she makes a bee line for the screen for a closer look.' When sleep overtakes her, Mollie can be found snuggling up on or under the master bed. She hates to be alone.

Mollie seems to settle with whoever is there, but, above all, Ernie is her favourite. 'In the house she will stay with me all the time. While sitting at my desk doing paperwork, Mollie is there under my feet waiting for the next walk. If she can work it she will manage to persuade me to go for four walks a day. Either a romp in the

© Js Library International

long wet grass, a stroll up the high street or a drive in the car. If anyone thinks of approaching her car she can turn quite aggressive and she'll bark them right out of the neighbourhood.'

'She can be extremely obedient. What I say goes most of the time! Unless I try to groom her – then she's heading for the door. She hates anything like that and tries to get away. If she gets the chance to wander off, you can bet she will.'

Mollie is full of plucky Scottie spirit with absolutely no fear. She fell into the swimming pool and managed to find her own way out; when she jumped on to the pool cover and found herself stranded in the middle, she waited patiently until she could be pulled off!

'When I was younger we could not afford luxuries. We did not keep a dog as we could not afford the licence fee, so we usually settled with a cat.'

Now Mollie has become a true family member. Should you one day come across Ernie, lead in hand, clambering and staggering down the river bank, you will find he is in hot pursuit of young Mollie. 'When I walk her by the river she sometimes clambers down the bank into the water, so I always make sure I have a collar on her so I can grab her!'

'She means everything to us. She is very important.'

~

Nikki & Sheba

*The two much adored German Shepherds belonging to
Health & Fitness Expert ROSEMARY CONLEY*

Rosemary Conley has become very well known for her continued success with her diet, health and fitness programmes and books. Her great belief is that one can keep fit with good, regular, fun exercise and healthy eating. But Rosemary has to admit that whilst one of her dogs is 'very fit', the other has become a 'bit of a glutton'!

Nikki and Sheba are Rosemary's two sable-and-black German Shepherds. Nikki is the mum, now eleven years old and Sheba, now nine, one of Nikki's eight puppies.

Throughout her life Rosemary has kept pets but these two are the first dogs her husband has owned and they have become very much a part of the family, adoring Rosemary's nineteen–year–old daughter. Says Rosemary, 'Our dogs are like our children. They are very special and we love them to pieces.'

'Nikki is very intelligent, very territorial and now very deaf! Whilst harmless when away from her home, she would certainly attend to an intruder and has done so! She has a good nip that says, 'I'm serious!' She is very fit for her age and has astounding energy. She is very lean and has an indifferent attitude towards food although she adores ordinary meat that we eat!'

'Sheba is more shy, is mentally backwards but very beautiful, gentle and loyal. She adores her food and will eat anything and everything. She has a total failing in this department! She has a tendency to gain weight because she is such a glutton! She once stole a whole frozen chicken that was thawing out at the sink and she ate the lot! There were no long term ill-effects but she didn't look well for the following few days!'

Both dogs adore Rosemary's company. 'They love being with us when we are in the house and they go almost everywhere we go.'

© Marc Henrie

They both adore their long walks, Sheba fetching sticks and they run happily off the lead ignoring other dogs. 'They would both however chase a cat despite the fact we used to have three of our own which they loved.'

When Rosemary and her family are away, she knows her dogs, especially Nikki, miss her. 'But so long as Sheba is with Nikki and they stay at home and go for plenty of walks, they are happy. We have a wonderful friend who house/dog-sits whenever we are away so they never have to go to kennels – they would think it was prison!!'

Obviously Rosemary would never be without her dogs. 'You're never alone if you have a dog,' she says. 'If either myself or my husband is away, the dogs provide us with someone to speak to, to "consider" and someone to comfort and love. They are the source of great joy and loyalty and add an extra dimension to our daily lives. Our two go to work with us and roam around the offices. The staff enjoy it and we all benefit I believe. The dogs get lots of strokes too. Yes, they are spoiled, but totally worth spoiling!'

~

Suzi

White Yellow Labrador belonging to
NICK OWEN, popular co-presenter of
BBC's 'Good Morning with Anne and Nick'

Six-year-old Labrador Suzi is 'Just Brilliant' says Nick Owen, when it comes to interacting with his own children.

Nick and his wife picked Suzi as a puppy because: 'We have four youngsters and Labradors are reputed to be so gentle with children.' Suzi never let her breed down and, 'She has now become a loving and loveable part of our large family.'

Nick is the dog walker in the family and as a result is Suzi's favourite person! When he is away she misses him very much. 'I take her for most of her walks. Open land on the Chilterns used to be our favourite until we moved away. Now Suzi loves the Lickey Hills near Birmingham. But as long as she can career off into the distance and then hurtle back again, Suzi is happy! She really enjoys a good run around with other dogs but is equally happy persuading the youngsters to join in her fun.'

Suzi was trained by Nick and he has ALMOST managed to remain the boss. 'She is reasonably well balanced and is now very obedient. She is very boisterous if encouraged, tossing around her favourite squeaky white bone, but otherwise she is happy to meander around the children and look longingly at anyone's food! She will eat everything and anything, including my slippers!!'

Alert and lively, Suzi is terrified rigid of hot air balloons and always reacts to something different going on. She guards her family and home and in return loves being pampered and treated as a family dog should be. Man's best friend? 'Yes,' says Nick. 'Suzi is incredibly loyal and devoted.'

~

© BBC

Jimmy The Cat

Much loved black tom owned by
GMTV Presenter LORRAINE KELLY

Television presenter Lorraine Kelly is unashamed to admit that she just LOVES cats! She helped to launch the Whiskas Champion National Pet Cat Competition on GMTV and took up her place as one of the judges at the final held in Central London. But she admits she found it extremely difficult to pick the winner as she quite simply fell in love with all the cats!

But there is one very special tom who shares her heart and will always come top of the list. Her own 'Jimmy The Cat'. Called Jimmy for short, he is a rescued black cat with a white tummy and white paws. Lorraine says: 'My husband Steve found Jimmy as a kitten in a refuge in the East End of London. Some cruel human had cut off all his whiskers. Steve immediately felt sorry for him and he's been with us ever since,' and she adds, 'all his whiskers have now grown back in!'

When Lorraine originally worked for TVAM, Jimmy became a feline long-haul passenger on the airlines, accompanying his mistress back to Scotland for the weekends. He flew from London to Edinburgh and travelled hundreds of miles by car but now he can purr with contentment as Lorraine and her husband have settled, for the time being anyway, in Berkshire.

'My Jimmy is such a placid cat. He never catches birds, never miaows but is always following me around purring very loudly like a wee motor bike. He loves getting his photo taken and his favourite pastime is eating dolphin-friendly tuna fish – and drinking French red wine.' 'But,' Lorraine quickly adds, 'it has to be French!!' Why is Jimmy The Cat so very special? Lorraine has four words to answer that – 'I just love him.'

~

© GMTV

Raq

Liver-and-white Springer Spaniel owned by
TERRY WAITE MBE and his family

Raq's claim to fame is his third prize in a local dog show. But he finds far more fun eating! He will eat anything, rummaging amongst the brambles to pick and eat his own blackberries, sampling the delights of green tripe, grapes and walnuts in their own shells – and cracking them himself, causing great amusement.

Unable to bring their black Spaniel into England from abroad, the Waite family bought Raq from a London kennel when he was a six-week-old puppy. Named after the Springer in the Romany Books on the Home Service Children's Hour, he was always eager to join in a game or two; rushing up and down the hall, jumping over whoever played with him. An excellent guard dog too, checking meter readers down the hall.

Terry's wife Frances takes Raq for his country walks, through long wet grass where Raq is in his element, swimming in rivers and lakes or off chasing rabbits, lifting his nose to catch the scents on the wind. 'But Raq has found it can be fun to turn a deaf ear when it suits him! On one occasion he fancied a walk on his own and trotted straight off across a main road disappearing for two hours of freedom.'

Frances remembers fondly how, when the children were small, Raq would sit on a chair by the window and watch them disappear off to school. 'He became a feature of the road and people would always look out for the gentle face with long soft ears peering out. Now, at a grand age and with arthritis, Raq is happy to live a quiet life. We will all miss him so much,' says Frances. 'Loyal, gentle and patient, Raq is one of the family.'

~

© Js Library International

Offa

A German Shepherd/Golden Retriever who became
DAVID BLUNKETT MP's very special Guide Dog

'Offa meant independence,' says David Blunkett, 'extra confidence, dignity and a substantial contribution towards being able to work on equal terms. He was a very big part of my life and an essential part of everyday living.'

Eight-year-old Offa — named after the King of Mercier a thousand years ago and Offa's Dyke — is a first time cross German Shepherd/Golden Retriever with a thick black-and-tan coat, who became a most faithful friend and guide to David Blunkett. The MP had already had two previous guide dogs — Ruby, a pedigree Labrador and Teddy, a curly-coated Retriever/Labrador. He joined forces with Offa when the dog was almost two. 'They all have different personalities,' David says, 'but they become your partner.'

Offa graduated from the Middlesborough Centre of the Guide Dog Association, having completed his guide dog training with flying colours. He had had specific additional training to deal with underground systems and peculiar working hours but after an adjustment period — David was very different in character to Offa's trainer — the pair got along magnificently.

Each day for Offa was as busy as the next — days sprawled out at home were few and far between! One day would be spent at the House of Commons in the MP's office, curled up in front of the door; then he would be off accompanying his master to every meeting and to all work activities, often into the Chamber. David believes he probably slept a great deal of the time in the meetings and committees (probably joined by some of the Members!). Offa became the only Guide Dog at The House of Commons — there were no previous members of The Commons or The Lords with guide dogs — and before David's dog Teddy, no guide was allowed in the Commons Chamber. Alongside his master, Offa proudly gained his promotion to the Front Bench!

'I think there was a great acceptance by other MPs being very helpful and friendly towards him,' says David, 'even if they did not agree with me!'

'Offa accompanied me on all constituency and out-of-London visits. I travel a great deal around the country by train and car. On the train, which I invariably use for weekly commuting, Offa would lie in the luggage rack behind the seats, where there is plenty of room!'

This dog was excellent at finding his way around the House of Commons but he was even better at finding his way to the parks! 'With Offa, I became slightly healthier,' David says, 'given the amount of exercise I had to do in giving him runs and keeping him healthy. His favourite game is chasing a ball or dragging gnarled sticks and old tree trunks through the woods, running free and chasing other dogs. On one occasion Offa charged between two ladies in the wood with a very long stick in his mouth – I think they thought they were being attacked!'

Offa can be extremely boisterous when he chooses, but very well behaved too. In fact, sometimes whilst with David, Offa was too obedient for his own good! 'Whilst out in the woods, I continued to call and call him away from another dog for two or three minutes, only to be asked by a fellow walker if I had a second dog. When I queried why, I was quietly told that Offa had been sitting next to me all the time I was calling!!'

David can not stress too greatly that feeding Guide Dogs titbits is just out of the question. 'It is absolutely crucial no guide should be fed anything other than his special diet, not just for the dog's physical well-being but because it would ruin them and make discipline and proper working arrangements frankly impossible.' Enforcing this rule is one of the biggest difficulties David has faced in having a dog.

Offa is an extremely strong and remarkable dog in terms of physique. But he has been very ill. A few years ago he was knocked down by a car, after being frightened by fireworks. During the General Election he had stomach torsions, where he was within

a whisker of losing his life. It was only his enormous strength and physical health which saw him through together with the excellence of the veterinary surgeons and staff.

And it's not just MPs who manage to get themselves into the tabloids. Offa found himself there when despite being in the front of a taxi queue, the driver declined to take him and his master to an engagement due to the fact he had an allergy to dog fur, and, guide dog or not, Offa's hair would get all over the velour seats. The next in the queue stepped into the taxi and Offa had to wait – famous master or not.

June '94 arrived and the time had come for Offa's retirement as an active guide. In the House the Health Minister took time out to wish him a long, happy and peaceful retirement. For David it was a very sad time. He knew he would miss Offa 'VERY much indeed'. He said, 'It would be impossible for me to keep Offa on as a pet when he retires because of travelling between London and Sheffield and the need to take on and care for a new dog. But on this occasion, something very special will be arranged for him.'

Offa now happily enjoys his retirement away from London, leaving David with a new guide-dog companion but still holding very fond memories for Offa, his ever-faithful guide and friend.

~

Tet

A cuddly Italian Spinone belonging to
Radio and TV Natural History & Wildlife Presenter
JESSICA HOLM (TV Co-Presenter of Crufts)

Ten-year-old Tet (Gaesten Amiamo Actero!) is an orange and white Italian Spinone, bred by one of the breed's pioneers in Britain. Spinones first came into the United Kingdom in the fifties but did not immediately become established. In the early eighties more were imported and their popularity established today's growing population. The breed standard says: 'Soft, almost human expression,' and that to Jessica Holm sums up her own Spinone. 'I fell in love with Tet at first sight,' she says 'Wouldn't you?'

'I have always owned dogs. Mongrels, an Irish Setter and a Dachshund as a child and as an adult three Spinoni, a Springer and a Cocker. Spinone Tet has become my intelligent, faithful companion, gentle, full of fun with a great sense of humour. As a puppy Tet was extremely accident-prone. He was always unzipping bits of himself on barbed wire fences but he has always been unbelievably brave and adores the vet despite an awful lot of treatment. He has made it through a whole series of operations on the tendons of his legs and also has crumbling elbows but you would never know it as Tet is in no way a hypochondriac! The result of all his operations has meant I only allow him lead walks on flat fields but in his mind he is galloping through forests with pheasant scent in his nostrils, waiting for the crack of gunfire!'

Jessica trained Tet herself from a very early age so he could accompany her on her squirrel research and he has always been a great support on dark nights and mornings when she had to check her live squirrel traps in spooky woods.

'When he was six months old Tet won Best Puppy at his first championship show and I continued to show him until he was two and a half years old by which time he had made two appearances at Crufts.'

© Andrew Gorman at David Wiltshire, Warminster

'He was also trained to do the job he was bred for and became the first Spinone in the United Kingdom ever to win an award at an All Breeds Working Test and one of the first to be run in Kennel Club Field Trials. He uses his brain and although I am the boss, he gently reminds me when he knows best!'

'Tet loves people but with other dogs he is not so sure. After he had got himself badly mauled by an Irish Wolfhound (who incidentally gave my mother-in-law a wound which required eight stitches for good measure!) with blood, spit and fur flying everywhere, now at the approach of other dogs, he tends to growl while his tail madly wags back and forth.'

Following in Jessica's footsteps, Tet has had his share of television fame. He has appeared in BBC's Wildlife On One in 'The Case of the Vanishing Squirrel', when Jessica was doing her squirrel research on the Isle of Wight and also on Clive Anderson's 'Notes and Queries' programme. 'But there is no pruning and pampering for Tet. He simply detests being groomed, loves to wade in swamps and has never had a bath in his life! It ruins the wire coat – which has a life of its own, dropping off all over the carpet all of the time but we don't mind!'

Other pets in the family include Poppy, a black Cocker Spaniel and Parrot Spike – a blue-fronted, hand-reared, Amazon Parrot who lives free in the house. Although Spike is top of the pecking order, Tet loves him and is in his element as he acts as a very effective hoover manoeuvring under the parrot's tree.

Jessica insists she will never see her dogs' welfare compromised. 'A friend will call every day when I am working to walk the dogs and whatever the plans are, the animals are always taken into account and placed on top of the list. Dogs don't replace human friends but they are the most rewarding extra friends. I couldn't be without them and in particular I can't imagine life without Tet. He means the world to me. He is simply THE BEST dog ever born!'

~

Muffin

Bearded Collie owned by world-famous
Wildlife artist DAVID SHEPHERD OBE

Muffin 'ScrumpleDumps' became a star. Full of mischief, this cheeky Bearded Collie acted as the model subject for various oil paintings by her master, world-famous wildlife artist David Shepherd — he of the 'stampeding elephants' fame.

After the death of a previous Old English Sheepdog, the Shepherd household were joined by Muffin, a creamy brown scruff! The Bearded Collie's character particularly appealed to David and what a character he found in Muffin.

Here was a real mischief-maker — soft and silly, wild and scatty, full of fun and life, totally single-minded and doing absolutely NOTHING that she was told to do! Was she trained? 'No way! You must be joking! Muffin was the Boss, single-minded and precocious yet equally lovable and adorable.'

In her thirteen years of ruling the Shepherd household, Muffin produced twenty-two glorious pups. The family kept one pup, Duffle, who became Muffin's inseparable companion even though she was totally the opposite to her mum, withdrawn and shy and more affectionate in her own way.

David feels he owes his loyal Muffin a lot. She produced a first beautiful litter of eight, all with their own special irresistible diverse characters who, at seven weeks old, had their portraits painted. Despite chaos, mayhem and pandemonium each and every feed time, David reluctantly let them go off to their new homes. His oil painting of 'Muffin's Pups' became the second-best-selling print in Britain that year and the print also appeared on cards sold in support of the David Shepherd Charitable Foundation, aiding conservation of wildlife and the habitat.

Oil painting and running the Conservation Fund keeps life at

Winkworth Farm hectic but Muffin knew exactly when it was time for a break. At exactly 10.30 a.m. she trotted in for coffee time in the farmhouse kitchen. 'She must have been equipped with her own built-in time clock. There on the kitchen floor she would sit with a 'don't forget me!' expression on her face, tilting her head to one side until it almost fell off. It couldn't fail to melt the hardest heart.'

'She understood English more than most people! Words such as "Walkies", even the letter *W* could not be mentioned in front of this intelligent canine. If she fancied a mad game, she would pinch every tea towel off the Aga. Then she would be off in search of her best friend, Rottweiler Diesel (who belongs to David's daughter) for a romp around the farm in search of squirrels. She tended to wander off on her own for hours on end, going walk-about, often returning at one in the morning with not a care in the world, covered in mud, clinging roots and brambles stuck to her coat as a result of persistent digging in the fields. She came and went as she pleased. After all, it was HER home!'

She certainly had her fair share of scrapes. 'She was involved in a car accident, where she fractured her skull, which left her one eyebrow-less – not that you would ever see under her wonderful scruffy mop of a fringe. She would accept pampering and attention all day if you offered it but try to groom her and she would get LIVID!'

After exhausting days, investigating everything and anything, Muffin would slump down on her British Rail cushion to snooze and dream – that is if she had not already managed to sneak into the bedroom and find the much more comfy bed!

'Last year Muffin had to be put to sleep due to cancer and in her last moments she just managed to become conscious enough to give a farewell lick to my wife and myself. She gave us thirteen wonderful years and was worth every wonderful minute. Having owned many dogs, Muffin was unique. She was a member of our family who meant everything to me.'

~

Tabitha & Leroy

Two Tabby Cats owned by
Naturalist Broadcaster & Writer ROGER TABOR

Roger Tabor, well known by all true cat lovers through his excellent BBC TV Series 'CATS', and his range of cat videos, offers his two special tabbies a most wonderful life.

'My two cats Tabitha and Leroy live with me in a watermill. It is a cat heaven – which they fully enjoy. Not only can they hunt in the fields and along the river, or bask in the sun on the old millstone and steps up to the door, but they also have the mill as combined playground and home. Although there has been a mill on the site since before Domesday, and parts of it are much older, the bulk of the building is two hundred years old and so is full of interesting hidey-holes for cats! There are old beams everywhere and wooden chutes that branch about like boughs on trees which make the best cat climbing-frame imaginable!'

'They are both tabby cats, but while Tabitha is a classic blotched tabby with its more freeform markings, Leroy has original wildtype narrow bands and spots just like his ancestors in ancient Egypt. Leroy also has some white on him which makes it easier for the non-technical tabby interpreter!'

'Leroy was originally a stray in South London, but he has adapted to his rural life as if to the manor born! He is very laid back in his approach to life but despite this he is a superb hunter. His theory seems to be: if it moves, catch it! He is a successful rabbiter, though his hunting each springtime makes no dent on the large local rabbit population. His skill even extends to catching moles that live underground! Remarkably on one wet night I remember him bringing in two in only half an hour!'

'Tabitha in contrast is a much shyer cat, and far less of an active hunter – although she is not averse to pinching Leroy's catches! She is more of a lap cat than Leroy and she instantaneously zooms

© Roger Tabor

on to my lap as soon as I sit down. Leroy will affectionately sit on my lap when he wants to, but is a great one for playing games.'

Roger's two tabbies are stars in their own right. 'Both cats are TV "superstars" having appeared in my BBC series CATS, shown in Britain and around the world from America to Australia, and in the book of the series. They also took the leading roles in my series of 'Cats on Film' videos. With this exposure, not surprisingly, they have their own following of dedicated fans who ask after them whenever I do a public appearance at a "cat venue".'

But these two felines are happiest when Roger is working from home. 'Both enjoy company and will accompany me on walks out into the nearby fields. When indoors, like all cats they love sitting on paper – and so are a great "help" when I am writing. Tabitha even "assists" with pieces so that I have to write around her shape!'

~

Rabbit

Tibetan Terrier/Jack Russell owned by
One of Britain's leading comedy actresses,
JUNE WHITFIELD OBE

In the past, if you were jogging or strolling along Wimbledon Common and happened to bump into June Whitfield, more than likely you would have seen her madly clanging metal discs and screeching, 'Rabbit! Rabbit!' at the top of her voice. But she wasn't, as you may have thought, in the middle of her latest comic role; she was in fact doing recall training with her sneaky terrier cross dog called Rabbit!

In possession of a terror terrier who loved to chase anything that moved – squirrels, cats, Dobermans, sheep and deer – June had resorted to calling in the dog-training experts.

She had spent many hours at a time, out in the country rummaging amongst the hedgerows looking for a sheepish, totally guiltless little face, until she discovered dog discs. As soon as Rabbit made a bee line after large hounds out on the common, a loud blast on a whistle and a mad jangling of metal discs turned a bounding dog into one frozen in his tracks! From then on, whenever June and her dog went for a walk, the discs went too and at the sound of their rattling – back trotted Rabbit.

June has always loved cats and never really took much notice of dogs until her husband Tim bought their first dog – Sid, a Golden Labrador puppy – into the home to join the family. Sid gave the whole family tremendous fun. He loved swimming so much June would have to dash past Wimbledon pond before letting him off the lead. Occasionally, temptation would prove too much and Sid would race back to jump and splash in the water! Not just swimming, Sid also loved to dig. June remembers: 'Sid totally disgraced himself by digging up the newly buried family tortoise on its funeral day!' A true family member, Sid lived to the good age of fifteen.

Sid wasn't immediately replaced and June's family went several years without another dog. Then actor Jimmy Edwards, with whom June was working on television, asked if she would mind looking after his dog Rubu (Swahili for moustache!) for a few weeks. Rubu was a cheerful, scruffy, crossbreed – his mum Dill, a Tibetan Terrier and his dad Dudley, a Jack Russell. Says June, 'Even dog experts were fooled by Rubu's breed. Barbara Woodhouse confidently told him he was a Norfolk Terrier!'

When Jimmy Edwards went off to Australia, June was not too keen on passing Rubu back and forth so she offered him her home for good.

'Often Rubu's name would get mistaken for Ruby, so Rubu officially became known as Rabbit,' says June. 'We became owners of the kind of cheerful, charming, scruffy crossbreed that gives mongrels a good name.'

June adores her dog, and gives him only the best. 'He loves smoked salmon and cheddar cheese – and then will promptly clean his whiskers on the best carpet. He loves to sprawl in front of the fire, loves to be a rascal barking in the garden late at night and trying to "kill" the hoover when it's on is a wonderful game.'

The worst thing of all, in Rabbit's opinion, is being left at home. He loves going for a car drive, sitting on June's lap in the front seat and looking out. Unless it's a motorway – too boring for this little chap. 'Yes,' says June, 'Rabbit certainly knows what he does and what he does not like, and believe it or not he HATES chocolate!'

June admits she 'couldn't ask for a more faithful friend' but, she says, 'We should remind ourselves that for every dozen dogs who live contented lives like Rabbit, there is one being mistreated by its owner or waiting to be destroyed because no-one wants it. We are supposed to be a nation of dog-lovers – we must all keep caring.'

~

Fozzy

Golden Labrador/Alsatian belonging to
Popular Entertainer RICHARD DIGANCE

Richard Digance tours the country entertaining packed audiences, while back at home with his family in Hampshire, eagerly awaiting his return, is his much loved dog.

'Fozzy is our Golden Labrador/Alsatian cross. He came from the Blue Cross Animal Rescue Centre at West End near Southampton, is five years old and is brilliant company for my two young daughters. Rosie, who is three, crawls all over him and he was an instant companion for the horse which my other daughter Polly rides.'

'When we went to look for a dog, with Fozzy it was love at first sight! He was very timid and scared of the other dogs so we reckoned he was due a reprieve. He very soon settled into his new home.'

'His favourite drink is what we are drinking! His favourite food is what we are eating! He loves cuddly toys and never goes anywhere without his soft rabbit. He loves long walks, chasing balls and sticks. He definitely seems to have taken to the Postman, although I am not sure that Postie appreciates Fozzy's interest!'

Richard is President of East London RSPCA. 'I think it is sad that so many dogs are discarded through no fault of their own. My last two dogs came from the Wood Green Animal Shelters in Hertfordshire and I have always gone to dog homes for our dogs, to try to help improve their lives and give them a second chance. Soon we will be out looking for another one to keep our Fozzy company.'

~

© Keith Curtis Photography, Hants

Daisy & Pansy

Two 'short-haired Moggies' belonging to
Radio and TV Presenter VALERIE SINGLETON OBE

Valerie Singleton fell into the trap all lovers of kittens fall into. Twelve years ago she offered a home to a little tabby-coloured kitten and ended up with a tiny Tortoiseshell-coloured one as well.

She remembers: 'A friend needed to get rid of her unwanted kittens and I liked the look of a little tabby one. But when I went back three months later to collect her, there was one other left. She was tortoiseshell-coloured and the runt of the litter no-one wanted. Yes – I ended up with two cats!'

The two kittens grew into 'plain straightforward short-haired moggies . . . but very pretty. I named the tabby 'Daisy', because she looks like a daisy! and the tortoiseshell 'Pansy'. Yes, she looks like a pansy!'

Both cats have their own individual characteristics. Daisy is the gentle, rather nervous one, not very good with strangers but enormously affectionate to Valerie and only then, in Valerie's company, does she feel totally secure. 'Daisy does like her food – she tends to be a bit fatter than she should be! I try out most things on my cats in the kitchen and it is quite amazing what they each like to eat. Apart from loving fish, Daisy chooses cheese, yoghurt, cereals, breads, Ryvita and pizzas! While Pansy, on the other hand, has her taste buds well tuned in to prawns!'

'Pansy is a clown! She is very sparky and a great flirt! She's affectionate and always nice to EVERYBODY and ANYBODY. Pansy is the curious one and the cat who is always in trouble!'

'Pansy has already used up three quarters of her nine lives. On one occasion she jumped from my balcony window ledge (in the crazy days when I thought cats never missed their footing or fell off anything). It was wet outside and I heard a scratching

sound. Looking out of my bedroom window I just saw two claws disappearing over the edge. It was a horrifying moment. There was I on the fourth floor and Pansy was falling into the basement below. Miraculously Pansy survived. On her way down she fell through the washing line (I found the two broken ends later), which must have helped to break her fall. The little cat broke her chest bone and punctured a lung. But she was still alive! She still has three knobbly bones protruding underneath – but they don't worry her at all. She still goes off seeking out trouble!'

Valerie would not be without these two little characters that share her home. 'Both like to be around me purring a lot. They roam the house jumping in boxes and searching out newly fresh tissue paper to lie on. Daisy likes any of my clothes and bags to hide in. Pansy likes to sit on the back of the chair in a room on the third floor so she can look out on the street below.'

'Daisy and Pansy are great company. They are always fun to watch. They will wait inside the front door to say *Hello!* when I return from a day's work. My two cats are never boring – they are quite simply special to me.'

~

Winston

Labrador/German Shepherd owned by
Professional ice-skater ROBIN COUSINS MBE
Olympic Gold Medallist 1980
Now running his own Ice Theatre Company in the USA

'I was never aware of animals and specifically dogs, until I had my own,' says Robin, whose opinions on dogs radically changed the day a ten-week-old Labrador/German Shepherd puppy was given to him when he moved to California.

Winston (named after Churchill, *not* a cigarette brand! insists Robin) was the pup of a rescued stray dog and has now grown into a fit and boisterous hound, somewhat coy, who all the time thinks he's human! 'He spends his time around people,' says Robin, 'loves to join in at parties, loves to give attention but most of all expects it in return!'

It is not a happy day for this beautiful large dog when Robin goes away. He will give his master the 'cold shoulder' whenever the suitcases make an appearance and he will promptly place himself down, right in the middle of one, to stop Robin from packing. Despite the fact that he knows the house-sitter well, it is not until two days after his master returns, when he is convinced that he is staying, that the dog will revert back to normal! Then back on form, it's back to the pool for a swim with Robin or a mad chase with his favourite tug toy.

'If there is anything sure to frighten this strong mighty dog,' says Robin, 'it is cowboy hats, earthquakes and Me . . . in a bad mood!' But Winston is an excellent guard dog. He will always protect his property and is a great alarm for visitors and trespassing animals. But once you've been allowed through the gate, your only danger is that of being licked to death!'

Robin says: 'Winston behaves most of the time but is a typical child. I *try* to remain the boss!' He did manage however to find

an excellent solution for Winston's thieving antics. The dog would frequently push the pantry door open and eat anything within range of his mouth – which meant everything! So, a few days later, someone hid inside the pantry and Winston was 'allowed' to repeat his venture. As his nose budged open the door, he got a very LOUD human surprise. Needless to say, Winston's nose has stayed well clear since!

Winston loves sitting on someone's knee – even though he is almost 100 lbs! But one person extremely grateful for Winston's size and strength was a painter working outside Robin's house. When the workman fell from his ladder and threw his back out, Winston ran straight over and allowed him to prop himself up for almost an hour without the dog moving an inch until he was able to crawl to the telephone inside.

Robin has kept three 'great' dogs. A few years ago, one of his students rescued a puppy from a plastic bag hanging on a supermarket door. The puppy, a Labrador cross was about two months old and a redhead, so was promptly named Fergie! She continued to stay with Robin but unfortunately one of her favourite habits was leaping the six-foot fence to freedom behind his home. Off she trotted round the gated neighbourhood and before returning, managed to find herself a friend . . . Two months later Fergie proudly produced four Labrador/Chow puppies! Fergie now lives in England with Robin's parents, who love her dearly. Robin says: 'Fergie is treated like a true Princess!'

But Robin did decide to keep one of Fergie's pups. 'I named him Thumper because that's what his tail does all day long!' Thumper and Winston are now totally inseparable friends. All the dogs are now fixed, speyed and healthy, and happy,' adds their master.

Robin feels his dogs' loyalty is 'quite staggering'. 'They have an uncanny knack of picking up various emotions and know when they can be loving and be your very best friend.' As for Winston: 'Winston means the world to me – I'd be lost without him.'

~

Mai-Mai & Dickie

A White Pekinese and a Black Labrador
'Two wonderful dogs' owned by
DAME BARBARA CARTLAND DBE, DStJ

Throughout the years Dame Barbara Cartland has kept many animals – cattle, a bull she loved dearly and many dogs, a popular favourite of hers being the Pekinese.

'My first Pekinese, Twi-Twi, was the only living dog ever to have been sculpted in Madame Tussaud's and he lived to the grand age of fifteen. When he went blind, running round in circles crying, the kindest thing to do was to put him to sleep.'

Pekinese Wong lived with Dame Barbara for sixteen years – a proud, independent and obstinate Peke but loyal, loving and whole-heartedly Dame Barbara's. In her words, 'Can anyone ask for more from a friend?'

Dame Barbara strongly believes that: 'What all animals need, which is very, very important, is the love that most people give them naturally. But some people forget they are like children and have to be continually reassured that they are wanted.'

When one of her dogs had cancer of the throat, it had to be put to sleep but it has never left her home. 'Despite the home previously being blessed, the ghost dog appears and still haunts my home today. Many people have seen him many times yet no-one is afraid. I know the dog was so happy, wanted and loved that it just does not want to leave it's home. The selfless love of any animal who has lived with us all his life is something which cannot be bought and is so precious.'

The two special dogs sharing Dame Barbara's home now are Mai-Mai and Dickie. Mai-Mai is a white Pekinese whose real name is Chiang Mai. She was bought to replace Twi-Twi just after Dame Barbara had visited Thailand. She says: 'White dogs are

very rare and difficult to come by – bitches are white; dogs usually beige. However, The Kennel Club having tried twenty breeders, eventually came across Mai-Mai. He is a very affectionate loving dog and if I go out for even just half an hour, Mai-Mai will greet me hysterically as if he is afraid he will lose me. When he sees boxes being packed for a journey, he never leaves my side and on my return will try to sit as close to me as he can on the bed and if possible on top of my face!'

Another popular breed with Dame Barbara is the Black Labrador. Her special friend Duke, a black labrador from the Queen's kennels at Sandringham, was given to her by Lord Mountbatten the Christmas before his assassination. Duke has now been followed by Black Labrador Dickie.

Dame Barbara is convinced that the reason her two dogs Mai-Mai and Dickie are so well is that she has always given them vitamins, herbal conditioners and tablets, crushed up and added to their food, containing bone meal, liver, seaweed and honey.

'A dog's company is so rewarding,' says the romantic novelist. 'So whenever possible Dickie and Mai-Mai accompany me. If they have to be left, two eager faces, one belonging to a black labrador, the other to a peke, will be waiting in the hall, thrilled at my return.'

Dame Barbara Cartland sums up in a couple of sentences how she feels about her two very special dogs. 'We must always remember when we take an animal into our home we are their world. Being with animals means contentment and a satisfaction that is greater than anything we can receive from another human being.'

~

My Dog and I

This poem was written by DAME BARBARA CARTLAND
About her Pekinese Wong, with her for sixteen years

For years you walked beside me every day,
   For years you slept upon my bed.
You showed your love in every way,
   I can't believe that you are dead.

If there's an after-life for me,
   Then I'd be lonely without you,
I must be sure that you will be
   With me, whatever I may do.

So I pray to God who made you and me,
   Who in death swept us apart,
To book a place in the 'Great To Be'
   For a dog with a loving heart.

~

Mitzi-Jo

A happy little Shih Tzu belonging to
Singer/Actress POLLY PERKINS who appeared in
The Spanish-based soap 'Eldorado'

Singer and Actress Polly Perkins has been a committed vegetarian for the past twenty years for the simple reason that she adores animals. She has lived in Britain, France and Northern Spain and with her work performing on the Spanish Club Circuit of the Costa del Sol, her home is now in Southern Malaga. Accompanying her always on her travels has been Mitzi-Jo.

About thirteen years ago Polly came across Mitzi-Jo. The little dog belonged to an opera singer and his wife who lived in Battersea, London, and as Polly was living in a flat at that time, she fell in love with her because of her compact size and more especially: 'Because she looked like a real dog and I could tuck her under my arm!'

'Mitzi-Jo is a very well balanced, happy dog. She loves visitors and always gives them a big welcome. She enjoys killing my slippers and often plays by rolling on her back and rubbing her beard with her paws. But most of all she loves working in front of television cameras!'

When Polly took on the part of Trish Valentine in Eldorado she remembers: 'Mitzi-Jo got her acting role alongside me by the skin of her teeth (in spite of not having many left now!). A Yorkshire Terrier was originally cast in the role but nepotism prevailed! . . . On one occasion in Eldorado we were shooting a scene which involved a heated argument. Mitzi-Jo was so upset that she ran off. She couldn't be found anywhere. There was a big hue and cry since we couldn't finish shooting the scene without her. We even thought she might have been kidnapped. Eventually she was found – in my dressing room – a long way from the set, curled up asleep! She proved her intelligence!'

As a youngster Polly grew up with Pekinese as family pets from

© BBC

where her love of dogs was born. Currently, as well as Mitzi-Jo, she also owns three cats and four other large dogs. But despite her lack of size, Mitzi-Jo is the leader. 'She likes chasing the cats and she bosses my other four larger dogs!'

Likey is Polly's Great Dane. 'She is now an old lady. I rescued her in Spain. She had been abandoned and I found her tied up to a tree in the full heat of the Spanish sun. She now has a touch of arthritis and in the winter she loves to come into the house at night and stretch out in front of the log fire!'

Likey teamed up with a neighbour's Mastiff and later with a Greyhound to proudly produce two sets of puppies, all of whom found good homes. Polly decided to keep pup Stormy from the first litter and pup Luther from the second. She also has one of Stormy's own pups Talulah (Tootsie for short).

Of her household full of hounds, Polly says: 'They all guard my house really well. Most nights they all sing to me at some stage! They are well cared for and very contented. I love them all dearly.'

~

Arthur Daley

The Great Dane owned by VERITY LAMBERT
Producer behind 'Cinema Verity'

Arthur Daley – a grand name for a grand breed of dog! This soft and gentle Great Dane, with the most wonderful expression on his face, has lived with Verity Lambert since the day she bought him from a breeder as a puppy. He has the most unusual, but beautiful, colouring of grey and white with black splodges and his name 'Arthur Daley' came from the television character in 'Minder', which Verity produced.

Unlike his namesake, this Arthur Daley has excellent breeding and makes the most of living the good life. He grandly travels, with his head held high, ears alert, looking out of the Mercedes window as he accompanies his mistress to work, then happily settles on his own bean bag in her Shepherd's Bush office for a long snooze. If a stranger arrives, he will turn on his wary expression despite everyone's eagerness to say 'hello' to the grand chap.

His loyalty will lie forever with his mistress. Verity trained her dog herself and the result is a most obedient dog with Verity remaining very much the boss in charge! But that does not mean that this, her third Great Dane, has not been able to get away with a trick or two in his time! She admits that: 'Arthur Daley has managed to eat his way through two sofas. On several occasions he has picked out and eaten the gas-fire coals spreading the bitten chunks all over the carpet, and on one particular day – obviously totally forgetting his breeding – he chose to be sick . . . in my handbag!' And despite having his very own bed, Arthur Daley can often be seen sneaking into his mistress's bedroom. Her bed is far more to his taste and with such pleading eyes, how on earth can Verity refuse?

Due to work demands, Verity must travel frequently, so often her dog is not able to keep her company. But he has many 'aunties' and 'uncles' only too willing to spoil him. When it comes to food time, he turns into a dog with a mind all of his own. The gentle

© Solo Syndication Ltd

giant is extremely fussy, but offer him any kind of biscuit, and you will be his best friend. But do not take him anywhere near a supermarket trolley when you go out to buy them – just one glance and he becomes a mass of trembling fear!

Arthur Daley loves to play. He keeps Verity on her toes, throwing and hiding his favourite toys – a squeaky cauliflower, a cracker and a miniature football. Outside he will 'go for a swim' in any type of water that he happens to come across and adores the fun of the chase – rabbits, squirrels and especially Labrador bitches! He's not keen on dogs with black fur but point him in the direction of a bitch with a black coat and he's away! 'On one occasion,' says Verity, 'he decided to leave my office, without letting me know, and took himself off to Shepherd's Bush Green on a bitch's trail!'

In a world of fast production schedules, programme meetings and finance, Verity's dog is a means of escape. She says, 'Arthur Daley means a lot to me. He is someone I can cuddle. He doesn't make demands and he never answers back!'

~

Hodge

Actress ALEXANDRA BASTEDO's
Special 'talking' Tonkinese

Alexandra Bastedo, Movie Star of the sixties, now lives with her husband in a seventeenth-century farmhouse near Chichester in West Sussex surrounded by her many animal friends. Despite still being a working actress, ducks and birds, dogs and donkeys fill her life and she will find time to rescue them all.

Alexandra has been on her farm now for over ten years and so began her interest in cats. Now there are seven and one of them has become her very special feline friend.

Grey tom Hodge, named after Dr Johnson's Library cat, is a ten-year-old Tonkinese. 'He is my "human" cat,' she says, 'and great company whether playing, talking or cuddling. He is incredibly affectionate, very very intelligent and has long conversations of questions and answers with humans. He talks to the birds so much they manage to get away. But he has been known to catch a moth – perhaps it couldn't hear!'

Hodge spent his early life shut up in an old lady's flat. He ended up in cat rescue where he was very antagonistic to all the other resident cats. When Alexandra first saw him she remembers: 'Hodge was extraordinarily beautiful, grey with lovely blue eyes. But he had specific difficulties. He hadn't been outside, he needed a children's diet but I felt we could cope.'

'We found Hodge has the FIV virus, which has a poor prognosis, but we feed him multiple vitamins and minerals daily to keep up his immune system and two years after the diagnosis, he is absolutely fine.'

Surrounding herself with animals, Alexandra takes her animal work very seriously indeed. 'There are sixty-one kittens at cat rescue locally right now needing homes. No responsible cat owner

should ever have an unneutered cat as hundreds of kittens are put down daily.'

Unlike his mistress, Hodge hates all her other animals! He is happy to spend his days curled up asleep in her bedroom or chattering away to anyone who will listen. In fact he NEVER keeps quiet.

'Because Hodge was waking us up too early for his breakfast,' says Alexandra, 'we bought a battery-operated food timer which we could set for 6.00 a.m. This worked fine for a week. Then Hodge decided 6.00 a.m. was not early enough. Bang! Wallop! Crash! it went around the room as he threw it about trying to open it up before time to grab an early breakfast. We're back to the vocal wake-up now.'

~

© Keith Curtis Photography, Hants

Dillinger

A Top Doberman belonging to
Top sportsman KRISS AKABUSI MBE

'He's big, he's bad, he's mad and he's musty!' states Kriss Akabusi about Doberman Dillinger.

'Dillinger is my second Doberman and I have had him for almost two years. He was born on my birthday, November 28 1993, and was a birthday present.'

'His pedigree name is Blitzgeist, which means lightning spirit, and boy, believe me, he is true to his name! Everything he does is fast. He runs fast, he eats fast and he barks fast. You may say, "How does a dog bark fast?" Well, he doesn't go "Woof! Woof! Woof!" He goes "WOOooOOOf!!!"'

'On a more serious note, my dog is very big and powerful. He would not do anybody any harm but he is obviously capable of it as he weighs more than seven stone and could be quite aggressive. That is why I think it is important to have dogs well trained and it is imperative that you have control over a dog this size. Dillinger is in the top class at Locksheath and District training club.'

'He is a great friend and is always really happy to see me. He is great fun and life wouldn't be the same without him.'

'He's my TOP DOG, Dillinger the Doberman!'

~

© Keith Curtis Photography, Hants

© Derek Tamea

Max

A strong German Shepherd for
Strongman GEOFF CAPES

A good strong dog was what strongman Geoff Capes was after and that's exactly what he got in his black/tan German Shepherd dog Max – who gained his name from the Mad Max film!

Geoff has always kept German Shepherds and bought Max as a puppy with an excellent pedigree. His father Jilrob had already proved himself at Crufts as Best of Breed. Max grew into an excellent guard dog. His barking would either warn you or welcome you. Geoff was always totally in control, trained Max himself to become loyal and obedient, often gentle . . . but sometimes totally wild!

Geoff laughs: 'He ate anything, liked bones but his favourite food was people! He loved to chase anything and everybody and totally disgraced himself by biting a good friend in the privates; not to mention the fight he had with next-door's bulldog!' Then in contrast Max would love to be gentle, stand still to be groomed, pampered and just be loved.

Max got on very well with Geoff's other dog, his German Shepherd bitch Mindy. Mindy managed to proudly produce one litter and Geoff managed to secure them all good homes, including three taken on for training by the police force.

For Max, master Geoff was his favourite. Holidays were waivered and Geoff says: 'I took Max everywhere I could. He loved to swim and get himself totally covered in black mud from the marshes just having fun.' Sadly, Max, after twelve years with Geoff, is no longer around. 'I felt a great loss when he died,' says his master. 'I could depend on him. He was a good friend. But there is satisfaction in knowing that he has offspring that give pleasure to others.'

~

© Js Library International

Basjan, (& Ronald, Atreyu, Pieter-Jon,

Jack, Angie & Jules!)

Olympic Athlete and World Cross-Country Champion
ZOLA BUDD's own canine pack!

Zola Budd Pieterse, International Runner, a member of the first South African team and living in South Africa, likes nothing more than talking about her animals. She just ADORES dogs! She was never without photographs of her much loved pets as she travelled to international races. At the last count she was the proud owner of seven dogs, three cats and a tortoise!

Collie cross Basjan is her particular favourite. She chose him in England from the Chobham branch of the RSPCA when he was two years old and took him back with her to South Africa in 1988. She reckons he has adapted extremely well, is a very obedient and clever dog and likes nothing better than his walks and runs in the fields, chasing hares and birds – providing there are no cyclists about, his one big fear – and fetching tennis balls. Basjan is the only one of Zola's dogs who does not chase her chickens – although he has been known to steal the odd piece of chicken from the table when no-one was looking!

Ronald (Zola's husband's dog) and Atreyu are the Rottweilers. They are extremely protective of their mistress and wonderful guard dogs. They will attack any stranger who comes on to their property but to Zola they are real softies. 'Ronald will lie right on top of me when I am watching TV, grabbing all my attention. He loves to hug me. He cannot stand my cats, just loves carrying tennis balls around.'

'Atreyu, on the other hand, ignores the television and prefers to watch the tumble dryer! She will sit entranced watching it for hours. Her favourite game is to attack anything that makes a noise, her two current favourites being the weed eater and the vacuum cleaner. One day she got herself in a right old mess when she fell into the

pool while snoozing on the patio! She has been a wonderful "mum", has had two litters, and I kept Pieter-Jon.'

The real terrors in Zola's family are Jack, Angie and Jules – three Scottish Terriers. Zola reckons they would take over if they had the chance, trying to copy the Rottweilers by guarding the property. 'They make the most awful lot of noise – purely for effect since they are extremely friendly!' They love people and always insist on the most attention. All three adore peanuts, popcorn and hunting for mice with a favourite game playing 'tug of war' with Zola's old running shoes. As for discipline – Zola maintains all her Scotties are a lost cause and have no discipline whatsoever! They decided to all go off missing together for two days and luckily were found in time. Then they stole some Christmas gifts and 'had a right royal time eating all the chocolates'!

Zola certainly has her hands full with all her animals but she would not have it any other way. All her dogs sleep in a Kennel outside and she does all the feeding and the walking herself. They all love their grooming sessions – Rottweiler Ronald so much so that he will steal the brush to get an extra go!

With Zola, running is no longer an obsession. A lot of the pressure has been taken off and she now does it because she enjoys it. Cross country, with no timing of laps and the most natural form of running, is her great joy. Whilst training, her dogs keeping pace beside her, she is at her happiest.

She will spend more money on her animals than she will on herself. 'I love to take care of them and to pamper them,' she says. She will miss classes so she can take them to the vet; she will miss training if one of them is ill and occasionally declines invitations to races because of them. 'Animals are my best friends,' says Zola. 'I adore dogs because they accept me for myself and best of all they do not read newspapers! I experience life through my animals. Through your animals you get a glimpse of how God intended us to act with love.'

~

Owen

Britain's best loved Astrologer
RUSSELL GRANT's typical Taurean dog

Six-year-old chocolate Labrador Owen Llantillo Plantagenet, otherwise known as Owen (Owain in Welsh!) but often called 'Odders!', 'Sausage Dog!', 'Poppet!', or 'Higgledy-Piggledy!', means THE WORLD to his owner, Russell Grant. 'He means as much to me as anything I can name that has blood and life in it!'

Russell has always loved animals. 'I've not always kept pets because mother and father were never very keen on them. My first pet was a black cat known as Amethyst, over twenty years ago and I've had many more pets since then. All my cats have been rescues.' Russell has a lot of links with Labrador Rescue Society, especially the Monmouthshire branch. His latest dog, Owen, originally born in Devon, comes from Hereford.

'Born on 12th May, Owen is a Taurean and a typical one at that,' says Russell. 'He loves his food and eats constantly, anything except sweet things. He doesn't like to move very much – you cannot get him off his bean bag once he's comfortable! He's not really into games, except for the occasional 'Tug'. He loves to walk but he doesn't like running!' Owen did have very bad hips but Russell took action to alleviate the problem and keeps him healthy.

'Owen has a host of friends. He usually prefers other dogs smaller than himself but his best friends are Anna, Peggy and Isla, all Labradors, and Ross an Alsatian, while his Best Friend of all is Roxanne the Border Terrier!'

'Most of all,' says Russell, 'Owen loves security and being in his home. I had a Sagittarian dog once and if you left the gate open, within half an hour one of the local shopkeepers would be phoning me up to tell me that my dog was there! But Owen never leaves anywhere without myself or my partner. He goes to my partner and

myself equally. When we are in different rooms, he will sit in the middle of both rooms, or spend time with one and then the other.'

'He is very loving and loyal. He won't budge from your side. If you go away he goes off his food. He's always pleased to see you and gives the same welcome whether you are back from the corner shop or New York!'

'Owen is quite simply incomparable to any pet I've ever had. THE BEST!'

~